Contents

S. Prakash Sethi, Zicklin School of Business, Baruch College,
The City University of New York (CUNY)

Lee E. Preston, and Danielle Mihalko,
Robert H. Smith School of Business, University of Maryland

Foreword

Since 1995 we, along with an international group of management scholars, have been engaged in a broad exploration and discussion of the role of the large corporation in modern, highly interdependent economies and societies. With financial support from the Sloan Foundation, this group became organized as the *Redefining the Corporation Project*.[1]

The goal of this project has been to develop a broad conception of the corporation as a vehicle for advancing the interests, and responding to the concerns, of multiple and diverse "stakeholders," defined as persons and groups that stand to benefit from, or be harmed by, corporate activity. We strongly believe that mutually satisfactory relationships with a wide range of stakeholders are a critical requirement for successful corporate performance over the long run. At an early stage in our project, we surveyed the existing literature and selected a group of contributions that reflected critical perspectives and issues (Clarkson, 1998). We also supported a number of narrowly focused empirical studies, some of which are currently being completed, presented and published.

It has been our intention from the beginning to develop a short statement of "principles" that would summarize the key features of "stakeholder management" as we have come to understand that term. It was our hope that such a statement of principles, along with its supporting commentary, could serve as a basis for discussion and for the evolutionary development and implementation of these ideas.

The current version of this statement and commentary are presented in this publication. We take responsibility for the final version of this material, which has been shaped by the comments of dozens of colleagues over a period of several years. Two related papers are also published here. One of these, by Professor S. Prakash Sethi, presents a strong case for the development and implementation of codes of conduct at company, industry and other appropriate levels of business activity. We are grateful to Professor Sethi for allowing us to reproduce this paper which he prepared originally for oral presentation. The second paper surveys and summarizes the most important broadly focused documents and proposals that have been issued in this field during the 1990s. (For a useful summary of company code contents and specific guidelines on development and implementation, see Clarkson, Deck and Leblanc, 1997.)

Probably no reader of the "Principles of Stakeholder Management" statement will be fully satisfied with its content. Some will find the wording bland, or seriously incomplete; others will find it argumentative or unrealistic, too far at variance with conventional managerial and legal rhetoric. We urge readers to consider the supporting "Commentary" carefully before making up their minds. We also ask critical readers to consider what, in their own opinion, *are* appropriate guidelines for managers confronted with the diverse performance criteria that determine both the legitimacy and the long-run success of business corporations in modern societies.

A project of this type is necessarily the work of many hands and minds. As various draft statements and commentaries have circulated through our network of international contacts over the past couple of years, several hundred comments and suggestions have been received and integrated in one way or another into our thinking. It would not be accurate to describe the result as a "consensus" among all these contributors, but the responses received so far have overwhelmingly supported the effort and the general concept, even though there are inevitably differences of opinion about details.

The overall design for this project, and the specific content of the "principles" document, has been strongly influenced by the contributions of the late Professor Max B.E. Clarkson, University of Toronto, who was one of its most influential initiators. In recognition of his contributions, and of the fact that the publication itself emerges from the Centre that bears his name, we have come to refer to these as the "Clarkson Principles." Important contributors to the final version of this document as it appears here, in addition to ourselves, include James E. Post, Allen Kaufman, and Michael Deck.

Comments and reactions to this document are welcome, and can be directed to the Clarkson Centre address shown on the cover, or to any of us individually.

We acknowledge with thanks the financial support of this entire project by the Alfred P. Sloan Foundation, and the helpful comments of its staff.

Special thanks are due to Lee Benson for her careful editorial work on this document.

Lee E. Preston *lpreston@rhsmith.umd.edu*
Robert H. Smith School of Business, University of Maryland

Thomas Donaldson *donaldst@wharton.upenn.edu*
The Wharton School, University of Pennsylvania

Leonard J. Brooks *brooks@mgmt.utoronto.ca*
Joseph L. Rotman School of Management, University of Toronto

References

Clarkson, M.B.E. 1998. *The Corporation and Its Stakeholders: Classic and Contemporary Readings*. Toronto: University of Toronto Press, Inc.

Clarkson, M.B.E., Deck, Michael, and Leblanc, Richard. 1997. *Codes of Ethics, Practice, and Conduct*. Hamilton, Ontario: Society of Management Accountants of Canada.

---

[1] The Project website is maintained by The Clarkson Centre for Business Ethics, and can be accessed at: http://www.mgmt.utoronto.ca/~stake/.

Principles of Stakeholder Management[1]

Introduction

The large, professionally managed corporation is the distinctive economic institution of the twentieth century. It has proved uniquely effective in mobilizing resources and knowledge; increasing productivity; and creating new technologies, products and services. Corporations have proliferated and grown because they meet the needs of various members of society: customers, workers and communities, as well as investors. The worldwide spread of corporate activity has produced an increasingly integrated and interdependent global economy.

The success of the corporation, however, inevitably gives rise to questions and criticisms. Corporations are spontaneous and voluntary associations in which diverse individuals and interests collaborate for the creation and distribution of wealth. Some critics question whether organizations with the vast scale and scope of contemporary multinationals *can* be effectively controlled and directed toward these purposes. Others are concerned about the limited range of interests directly represented in corporate governance, and the lack of openness in corporate decision-making. And, as multinational corporations expand their activities and linkages, both corporate managers and their critics search for **principles for action** that transcend national borders and cultural values, and **modes of operation** that will achieve the broad purposes of the corporation on a long-term and sustainable basis, without undue conflict with diverse human and social norms.

The "**Principles of Stakeholder Management**" presented in this document have been developed in response to these concerns and needs. They are addressed to "managers": those individuals at any level who are responsible for the performance and impact of the corporation. They are consistent with the basic organizational structure and purpose of the modern business enterprise; they do not suggest that the corporation be turned into a "polity" (i.e., a unit of political government), nor into an agency of the state. In sum, these guidelines are intended to make managers more aware of the diverse constituencies that they are obligated to serve and increase the openness of management processes.

There are many reasons to believe that adoption of a "stakeholder" approach to management will contribute to the long-term survival and success of a firm. Positive and mutually supportive stakeholder relationships encourage trust, and stimulate collaborative efforts that lead to "relational wealth," i.e., organizational assets arising from familiarity and teamwork. By contrast, conflict and suspicion stimulate formal bargaining and limit efforts and rewards to stipulated terms, which result in time delays and increased costs. In addition, more and more executives are recognizing that a reputation for ethical and socially responsible behavior can be the basis for a "competitive edge" in both market and public policy relationships. Finally, in spite of the specification and measurement difficulties involved, many research studies have found evidence of positive associations (and few have found negative associations) between various socially and ethically responsible practices and conventional economic and financial indicators of corporate performance (profitability, growth, etc.) Thus, there is no reason to think that the conscientious and continuing practice of stakeholder management will conflict with conventional financial performance goals.

The Stakeholder Concept

The constituencies that are affected—favorably or adversely—by the operation of the corporation are referred to here as its "stakeholders." The implication of the term is that such parties have a "stake" in the corporation: something at risk, and therefore something to gain or lose, as a result of corporate activity. Many stakeholders (e.g., investors, employees) are linked to the corporation through explicit contracts. With many others (e.g., customers), contractual relations may be largely implicit, and subject to specific interpretation only in problematic circumstances. Still other interests—third parties outside the network of explicit and implicit contracts—are non-contractual and often involuntary, and the parties involved may even be unaware of their relationship to the corporation until some specific event, favorable or unfavorable, draws it to their attention. Impacts on third parties are often referred to as "externalities," because they occur outside the range of the firm's internal and market relationships. Examples of third party impacts are economic benefits or environmental harms that may be experienced by communities as a result of corporate operations. Such impacts, although clearly "external" to the firm as an organization, are nonetheless real, and perhaps significant: they are, therefore, within the normal purview of responsible management. The notion that important aspects of corporate performance can be ignored by managers because they are "external"—perhaps as a result of being deliberately "externalized"—is incorrect.

The Status of Shareowners

Shareowners have a special status among stakeholders in that their potential gain or loss from their involvement with the corporation is determined as a residual: it depends upon what is "left over" after all other stakeholder claimants have received their specified distributions. If a firm is, or is expected to be, profitable, its shareowners may receive dividends or appreciation in the value of their shares; if a firm incurs, or is expected to incur, losses, its shareowners will correspondingly lose. (Of course, other contractual stakeholders may be included in profit-sharing arrangements, and even non-contractual third parties (e.g., philanthropies) may benefit or suffer because of variations in corporate profitability.)

The distinctive position of shareowners among stakeholders is not due to their fractional "ownership" interest in the corporate entity, which is essentially a legal artifact; and owning stock is not "riskier" than other forms of association with the corporation. Indeed, the possibility of job loss (to employees), product failure (to customers), etc., may be much more significant to the parties involved than the impact of any single corporate bankruptcy on a well-diversified shareowner. But employee and customer risks (like the risks of lenders) arise because the corporation may fail to fulfill its contractual obligations. By contrast, shareowner risks are an inherent feature of their "ownership" contract. They have agreed to take whatever is left over, or the current market value of whatever is expected to be left over in the future.

The Legal and Moral Duty of Managers

Managers occupy a special place within the corporate structure. They are responsible for negotiating contracts with the firm's voluntary constituents and for accommodating the firm's involuntary stakeholders, in order to turn these disparate individuals and groups into a cooperative, wealth-enhancing network (or, at least, to minimize the number and severity of unavoidable conflicts). They attempt to accomplish this task by distributing among stakeholders the rewards and burdens that arise from corporate activity in ways that encourage (or at least do not discourage) their participation and by developing organizational processes and cultures that enhance stakeholder satisfaction.

The responsibilities of managers require and presume discretionary authority, and, as a condition of this authority, managers owe the corporation a duty of loyalty. This duty is, to some extent, a matter of law. But the moral responsibility of managers exceeds the normal market standard of indifference (i.e., not knowingly doing harm) and embraces all of the stakeholders of the firm, not merely the shareowners. Managers have an obligation to deal openly and honestly with the firm's various stake-

Principles of Stakeholder Management

Principle 1	Managers should **acknowledge** and actively **monitor** the concerns of all legitimate stakeholders, and should take their interests appropriately into account in decision-making and operations.
Principle 2	Managers should **listen** to and openly **communicate** with stakeholders about their respective concerns and contributions, and about the risks that they assume because of their involvement with the corporation.
Principle 3	Managers should **adopt** processes and modes of behavior that are sensitive to the concerns and capabilities of each stakeholder constituency.
Principle 4	Managers should **recognize the interdependence** of efforts and rewards among stakeholders, and should attempt to achieve a fair distribution of the benefits and burdens of corporate activity among them, taking into account their respective risks and vulnerabilities.
Principle 5	Managers should **work cooperatively** with other entities, both public and private, to insure that risks and harms arising from corporate activities are minimized and, where they cannot be avoided, appropriately compensated.
Principle 6	Managers should **avoid altogether** activities that might jeopardize inalienable human rights (e.g., the right to life) or give rise to risks which, if clearly understood, would be patently unacceptable to relevant stakeholders.
Principle 7	Managers should **acknowledge the potential conflicts** between (a) their own role as corporate stakeholders, and (b) their legal and moral responsibilities for the interests of stakeholders, and should address such conflicts through open communication, appropriate reporting and incentive systems and, where necessary, third party review.

holders and to avoid purely self-serving actions which their privileged access to information and discretionary authority may make possible. Managerial policies and processes should emphasize the *interdependence* among all stakeholders and should demonstrably reflect the application of a common standard of *fairness*.

Commentary on the Principles

*Principle 1: Managers should **acknowledge** and actively **monitor** the concerns of all legitimate stakeholders, and should take their interests appropriately into account in decision-making and operations.*

The first requirement of stakeholder management is an awareness of the existence of multiple and diverse stakeholders, and an understanding of their involvement and interest in the corporation. Many stakeholders — investors, employees, customers—are readily identified because of their express or implied contractual relationship to the firm. Others may identify themselves because of the impact, positive or negative, of the firm's activities on their own well-being. And, of course, some third parties may claim a "stake" in the firm when no such relationship, in fact, exists. Managers are not obligated to respond favorably to every request or criticism; they are, however, obligated to examine all such claims carefully before passing judgment on their validity.

The salience of specific stakeholder concerns varies among different areas of managerial decision-making, and according to the time horizon involved. Current working conditions are of greatest concern to employees; the cost and quality of products are of greatest concern to customers. Long-term survival and growth may be of greatest concern to investors and to the communities within which the firm operates. In taking particular decisions and actions, managers should give primary consideration to the interests of those stakeholders who are most intimately and critically involved.

*Principle 2: Managers should **listen** to and openly **communicate** with stakeholders about their respective concerns and contributions, and about the risks that they assume because of their involvement with the corporation.*

Communication, both internal and external, is a critical function of management, and effective communication involves *receiving*, as well as *sending*, messages. Hence, to understand stakeholder interests and to integrate various stakeholder groups into an effective wealth-producing team, managers must engage in *dialogue*. A commitment to engage in dialogue, however, does not constitute a commitment to collective decision-making: there are obvious limits as to the amount and content of information—particularly information about strategic options under consideration—that can be appropriately shared with particular stakeholder groups. Nevertheless, the more open managers can be about critical decisions and their consequences, and the more clearly managers understand and appreciate the perspectives and concerns of affected parties, the more likely it is that problematic situations can be satisfactorily resolved. Open communication and dialogue are, *in themselves*, stakeholder benefits, quite apart from their content or the conclusions reached.

> *Principle 3: Managers should* **adopt** *processes and modes of behavior that are sensitive to the concerns and capabilities of each stakeholder constituency.*

Stakeholder groups differ not only in their primary interests and concerns, but also in their size, complexity, and level of involvement with the corporation. Some groups are dealt with through formal, and even legally prescribed, mechanisms, such as collective bargaining agreements and shareowner meetings. Others are reached through advertising, public relations, or press releases; still others (e.g., government officials) are reached largely through official proceedings and personal contacts. Both the mode of contact and the type of information presented, or the opportunity for dialogue, can appropriately vary among different stakeholder groups, although the descriptions of situations and explanations of actions offered by managers should be consistent among all stakeholders. Extreme caution is required when managers deal with stakeholder groups that have limited capacity to assimilate and evaluate complex situations and options.

> *Principle 4: Managers should* **recognize the interdependence** *of efforts and rewards among stakeholders, and should attempt to achieve a fair distribution of the benefits and burdens of corporate activity among them, taking into account their respective risks and vulnerabilities.*

A business firm is a purposive organization in which all voluntary stakeholders collaborate for mutual benefit. Involuntary or consequential stakeholders (e.g., communities or third parties) may also be affected by the operation of the enterprise. And both voluntary and involuntary stakeholders are vulnerable, and *differently* vulnerable, to the effects of uncertainty and change over time. Successful managers will see that all stakeholders receive sufficient benefits to assure their continued collaboration in the enterprise, and that their burdens and risks are no greater than they are willing to bear. Again, the openness and demonstrable fairness of the distribution of benefits and burdens among stakeholders are, *in themselves*, stakeholder benefits. Managers may need to make special efforts to demonstrate stakeholder interdependence and the collaborative nature of the enterprise to non-contractual and involuntary stakeholders.

> *Principle 5: Managers should **work cooperatively** with other entities, both public and private, to insure that risks and harms arising from corporate activities are minimized and, where they cannot be avoided, appropriately compensated.*

Corporate wealth creation necessarily gives rise to consequences that may not be fully mediated through the marketplace. Some of these may be beneficial and welcome; others may be harmful. Monitoring and ameliorating undesirable consequences (i.e., "negative externalities") often requires cooperation with other firms, private sector organizations, public agencies and units of government. Managers should be proactive in developing contacts with relevant groups and in forging coalitions aimed at reducing harmful impacts and compensating affected parties. The often true observation that "one firm cannot solve this problem alone" should be a stimulus to multi-party cooperation, not an excuse for neglect and inaction.

> *Principle 6: Managers should **avoid altogether** activities that might jeopardize inalienable human rights (e.g., the right to life) or give rise to risks which, if clearly understood, would be patently unacceptable to relevant stakeholders.*

The ultimate consequences of most human endeavors—particularly endeavors involving large expenditures, diverse interests and long time periods—can never be fully anticipated in advance. Hence, managerial decisions and corporate operations necessarily give rise to multiple and diverse risks. Managers should communicate openly with stakeholders concerning the risks involved with their specific roles in the corporate enterprise, and should negotiate appropriate risk-sharing (and benefit-sharing) contracts wherever possible. When stakeholders knowingly agree to accept a particular combination of risks and rewards, then the arrangement is usually considered satisfactory. However, some projects may have consequences for which no conceivable compensation would be adequate, or risks that cannot be fully understood or appreciated by critical stakeholders. In these circumstances, managers have a responsibility to restructure projects to eliminate the possibility of unacceptable consequences, or to abandon them entirely if necessary.

*Principle 7: Managers should **acknowledge the potential conflicts** between (a) their own role as corporate stakeholders, and (b) their legal and moral responsibilities for the interests of all stakeholders, and should address such conflicts through open communication, appropriate reporting and incentive systems and, where necessary, third party review.*

Up to this point, we have spoken of managers as if they were disinterested coordinators of stakeholder interactions. However, managers also form a distinct stakeholder group, with privileged access to information and unique influence on corporate decisions. As stakeholders, managers are naturally interested in the security of their jobs, the level of their rewards, and the scope of their discretion in the use of corporate resources. Other stakeholder groups—shareowners and boards of directors, in particular—have devised a variety of arrangements intended to align the interests of managers with those of the corporation as a whole, and to prevent opportunistic abuse of managerial positions.

However, the tension between the interests of managers as stakeholders, on one hand, and those of other stakeholder groups and of the corporation itself as an on-going entity, on the other, is unavoidable. Responsible managers will recognize this, and will therefore accept and encourage organizational practices intended to control this source of intra-organizational conflict. Managers gain credibility when they establish procedures to monitor their own performance and, when appropriate, to facilitate third party review. Credibility matters when managers ask other stakeholders to align their interests with those of the corporation, and to act responsibly rather than opportunistically. Without mutual credibility, stakeholder trust diminishes and the collaborative character of the organization may be jeopardized.

---

[1] This document, based on comments and suggestions from many participants of the *Redefining the Corporation Project,* was developed by Max B. E. Clarkson, Lee E. Preston, Thomas Donaldson, and Leonard J. Brooks.

Principles of Stakeholder Management

Codes of Conduct for Global Business: Prospects and Challenges of Implementation

S. Prakash Sethi, Zicklin School of Business, Baruch College, The City University of New York (CUNY)[1]

Corporate Codes and Critics

In the United States and Western Europe, corporate codes of conduct have become *de rigueur* for most large corporations. According to recent studies, 60 to 70 percent of major US corporations have issued codes of conduct, and many of the largest foreign multinationals have done so as well. These codes usually attempt to state the company's mission, values, and goals, and to describe its relationship to various stakeholders, both internal and external. Unfortunately, most of these codes suffer from a number of flaws:

- They are presented as public statements of lofty intent and purpose, but lack specific content.
- While they mention the corporation's commitment to its customers, employees, etc., they ignore the *rights* of these key stakeholders in their dealings with the company.
- They make no provisions for internal implementation, and code compliance is not integrated into the organization's procedures and reward structure; hence, managers and employees are often uninformed about the codes and their content, and do not take them seriously.
- They provide no basis or framework for communication with external communities about the efforts and results (success or failure) of the corporation in achieving the codes' objectives.

The inevitable result of these defects is that corporate codes of conduct are often treated with disdain by knowledgeable and influential opinion leaders among various stakeholder groups, as well as by outside analysts and the public at large. To be sure, there are a handful of companies whose codes of conduct are taken more seriously by their constituencies. Notable examples are those of Motorola, Levi Strauss, Texas Instruments, Sara Lee, and Mattel. However, the very smallness of this group reinforces my point. And, with the exception of Mattel, none of these corporations has chosen to make public either the process by which it seeks compliance of its code within its own organization (particularly by its overseas subsidiaries and strategic partners), or the results of its compliance efforts. Nor have the corporations, with the exception of Mattel, subjected their codes or processes to independent outside verification.

The weakness of corporate commitment to code compliance is all too apparent. After thirty years of research and teaching in this field, I can point to only one major corporation that has asked external independent monitors to examine its code compliance and has made the results public. This example is Nestlé, the Swiss-based multinational corporation and one of the world's largest manufacturers of food and related products. Nestlé was confronted with worldwide public boycotts of its products, and demonstrations by advocates of the poor and developing countries for its alleged improper marketing and promotional activities in the sale of infant formula products in these countries. Although inherently safe, these products were too expensive and largely unnecessary in these settings. Poor and uninformed mothers in developing countries were pressured into buying these products through intense promotion. Eventually, the World Health Organization enacted an International Code of Marketing of Breast-Milk Substitutes (Infant Formula Code) which banned most advertising and promotion of such products. Nestlé was strongly opposed to the development of this Code. Nevertheless, after the Code was enacted, Nestlé announced its willingness to abide by the Code and arranged for independent verification and compliance monitoring. The outcome was highly salutary. Within a period of less than four years, Nestlé's reputation was largely restored, and the boycott against the company's products was called off.

Since that time, only one US multinational corporation has voluntarily promulgated a global code of conduct that committed itself to independent monitoring by an external group of credible and experienced persons charged to make a public report of their findings. That company is Mattel, one of the world's largest producers of children's toys including Barbie, Hot Wheels and Fisher Price products. This experience, and my personal involvement in it, will be further discussed below.

Corporate Response to Criticism
There have, of course, been a few other notable positive responses by major corporations, both individually and collectively, to public criticism. The promulgation of the Sullivan Principles by US firms operating in

S. Prakash Sethi

South Africa is a significant example. For the most part, however, multi-national corporations have responded to public pressures in two less-effective ways:

- They claim to abide by all local laws and standards. They also declare that their practices are driven by competitive market forces, low worker productivity, and the extra cost of doing business in different countries. Furthermore, they claim, often with some justification, that wages and working conditions in their own plants are superior to other plants in these areas.
- They promulgate voluntary codes of conduct that appear to address the concerns of their critics. Unfortunately, these weak and haphazard efforts often reveal the *absence* of long-term strategies to deal with underlying issues, as well as inadequate programs of public communication. Very few companies have created codes of conduct or "best practice" by which they can actually guide and evaluate their overseas operations, or the conduct of their local partners and suppliers.

Companies are often seen as being dragged into action only when public pressure becomes too intense to ignore. Alternatively, companies have resisted change by spending incredible amounts of time and effort in discussions about code formulation. This can be seen in the case of the apparel industry's code of conduct. President Clinton announced this initiative with great fanfare in June, 1997, but only after many years of intense public pressure. It then took almost eighteen months for the various parties to come to a specific agreement about what would be audited, who would do the auditing, and what type of report would be published. As a result of these delays and disagreements, the entire process is viewed by the public with great skepticism. As a matter of fact, two of the leading public interest group participants in the negotiations have refused to sign the new accord and have denounced it as too weak. Moreover, if experience to date is any indication, the implementation process is also likely to be subject to intense discussions among the participants, with resultant delays. Thus, it will be quite some time before anyone will have an opportunity to evaluate the importance and effectiveness of this code. The consequence of these failings has been further public antagonism and pressure on the corporations. Thus, rather than gaining public support and recognition for their efforts, the companies involved are being denounced for bad faith. There are also efforts to pursue legislative and regulatory approaches at national and international levels that would compel companies to undertake desired actions.

The Imperative of Global Codes of Conduct

Let me state categorically and unequivocally my belief that corporate codes of conduct are here to stay. Further, they are both necessary and desirable. When properly developed and implemented, codes of conduct can provide the corporation with a voluntary and flexible approach to addressing some of society's concerns, both in general and in the market-place. Codes can serve both corporate interests and public purposes and can strengthen free market institutions, as well. Effective use of codes can restore public faith in the market economy as the best avenue for enhancing human welfare, advancing regional economic development, and strengthening democratic institutions.

Public sentiment and perspective play a very important role in defining the parameters of discretion that a society will allow the leaders of its various social, political, and economic institutions. In the present instance, as well as in many previous instances involving social issues, the fight for the hearts and minds of the public have invariably been led by corporate critics. Companies, fearing lack of public trust, have refrained from a proactive stance and have instead limited themselves to disputing their critics' charges. This is a losing battle and will always remain so. By yielding the initiative to their critics, companies have allowed their critics to shape the agenda in ways that put business in a perpetually defensive mode, talking about "what they may have done wrong" instead of "what they are doing right."

Codes of conduct offer an invaluable opportunity for responsible corporations to create an individual and highly positive public identity for themselves; that is, a reputation effect that can have a direct result on their bottom line in terms of increased revenues, customer loyalty, expanded markets, a productive work force, and a supportive political and regulatory environment. Furthermore, an increased level of public confidence and trust among important constituencies and stakeholders would lead to greater freedom for management in the running of their business operations, and insulate them from the actions of other, less scrupulous firms in the market-place.

Voluntary codes serve to achieve a larger public purpose in a manner that is flexible and pragmatic and take into account the unique set of problems faced by an industry or by different companies. They also allow the moderate elements among the affected groups to seek reasonable solutions to the issues involved, even before these issues are captured by more radical elements whose primary interest may be in escalating the level of social conflict, rather than fashioning mutually acceptable and feasible solutions. And they avoid the need for further governmental regulation that is invariably more expensive and less efficient (because of political considerations and the need to create regulations that cover all possible situations and contingencies).

Creating a Code of Conduct

The remainder of this paper is devoted to a discussion of the development and implementation of a meaningful code of conduct for globally active corporations. This discussion will draw on my own experience as chair of the Mattel Independent Monitoring Council for Global Manufacturing Principles (MIMCO).

Characteristics of a Viable Code

A corporate code of conduct is in the nature of "private law" or a "promise voluntarily made," whereby an institution makes a public commitment to certain standards of conduct. The fact that issuance of a code is "voluntary" reflects the flexibility of action afforded to a corporation. Commitment to a code affirms that corporations and their critics share a common interest in improving the conditions of their interaction, and in mutually satisfactory resolution of underlying issues.

For a code of conduct to have any reasonable chance of meeting the expectations of all parties involved, the following conditions must be met.

- The code commitments must be economically viable for the corporation, given the dynamics of its technology and competition, and the economic and sociopolitical realities of the environments within which it operates.
- The code must address substantive issues that are of importance to the corporation's various constituencies, particularly employees, communities, and governments.
- The code must be specific about performance standards that can be objectively measured.
- Important constituencies of the corporation must be engaged in the code formulation and implementation process.

Development and Implementation

Development and implementation of a multinational code of conduct is a challenging task because of the differing orientations and concerns of the diverse parties involved; their disparate assumptions about the feasibility of particular goals and benchmarks; and disagreements about the means that are appropriate and feasible to achieve agreed-upon goals. Another major hurdle arises from the organizational ethos and decision-making processes of corporations and other participative and public interest groups. A corporation's primary focus is on the efficiency of processes and the optimization of outcomes. Participative and deliberative processes, e.g., open consultations and procedural norms, are adopted only as means to achieve desired ends and are not seen as values themselves. By contrast, many stakeholder groups place tremendous importance on consultation and information sharing, not only as steps in effective decision-making, but as values themselves. Thus, from their perspective, efficient use of time and resources may take second place to consultation and involvement; and corporate actions that appear to jeopardize participative processes are viewed with distrust.

Assuming that there is adequate commitment to widespread participation and involvement in code development, the next step is to determine the **scope** of the proposed code. This includes:

- Definition: What aspects of corporate activity and impact are to be included in the code?
- Measurement and Verification: How should corporate performance in these areas be measured, and how should the accuracy of this information be verified?
- Accountability and Reporting: To whom should the corporation be accountable for its performance, and how should this information be made public?

Specificity in all of these matters is critical because an ambiguous code tends either to become meaningless, or to expand into varied meanings as different groups stretch its terms to suit their particular interests. Code requirements must be translated into quantifiable and standardized measurements so that objective and consistent observations can be made by different people, over time. Code compliance must become an element of management routine that is integral, rather than peripheral, to the firm's normal operations. And, most importantly, indicators of code compliance must reflect results rather than intentions: goals met or unmet, not merely actions taken in pursuit of goals.

Two final points on implementation are these:

- The company's top management must be strongly and unequivocally committed to the code, and code compliance must be an element of performance evaluation at all levels of management.
- The company must be willing to expose its record of code compliance to external verification. This last step is particularly important if the firm expects to achieve "reputation effects" and the benefits of stakeholder trust and collaboration, as well as public approval.

Independent Monitoring Systems
One of the most critical aspects of code implementation is the creation of

S. Prakash Sethi

an independent monitoring system. Independent monitoring is necessary for the public to see that companies are indeed doing what they proclaim to be doing. Unfortunately, most companies with codes are extremely reluctant to subject themselves to independent outside monitoring and public dissemination of monitoring results.

This is an area of great disagreement between corporations and their critics, and a major source of public distrust about corporate motives and performance. Reluctance to share information is sometimes justifiably based on the fear that the company will be subjected to inappropriate pressure and harassment, rather than be applauded for the progress it has made. However, inadequate disclosure inevitably suggests that there is something to hide, and suggests a lack of faith in the ability of stakeholders to appreciate and encourage good corporate conduct. It is ironic that corporations expect their financial performance to be publicly reported and audited by independent outsiders for the benefit of investors, but are unwilling to provide other information—often much less sensitive—of comparable concern to other vital constituencies.

Companies have often argued that many indicators of code compliance are internal measures, not conventionally subject to outside review, and that confidentiality makes it easier to take corrective actions through a system of "carrot and stick." This line of argument, however, has not been successful in previous situations involving crises of public confidence and is doomed to failure in the current global socio-political environment. Neither advanced nor developing countries will allow companies to operate any longer under a "veil of secrecy" where issues of human rights and ethical/moral conduct are concerned.

There are currently two approaches to creating and implementing codes of conduct with appropriate performance verification and public reporting processes. One involves industry-wide effort; the other suggests that individual companies should develop their own approaches, based on their unique circumstances. We briefly consider the advantages and disadvantages of each.

Industry-Wide Effort
The case for an industry-wide effort is based on the premise that companies in an industry face similar sets of problems, competitive conditions, and external pressures. Therefore, a combined approach should be feasible, cost effective, and place all companies on the same competitive footing with respect to these issues. An industry-wide approach also gives participating companies a united position with which to respond to their critics and public at large.

There are, however, serious flaws to this logic:

- An industry-wide approach requires consensus before any action can be taken. It therefore plays into the hands of those companies who are least inclined to undertake substantive action, and thus can postpone implementation through endless discussion, procrastination and obfuscation, thereby defeating the purpose of the exercise and inviting public ridicule and distrust.
- It forces industry performance standards to the lowest common denominator; i.e., the company with the weakest record sets the pace for the entire industry.
- It reduces incentives for individual companies to improve their own performance based on their own particular circumstances.
- Since these industry-wide efforts invariably depend on "voluntary compliance" and rarely incorporate monitoring or enforcement measures, poorly performing companies remain undisciplined and taint the record of the entire industry.

I do not believe that, at the present time, an industry-wide approach is either feasible or desirable in most cases. Since very few industries have even a modicum of "commonly accepted" standards or performance criteria in *any* area of public concern, an effort to develop common performance criteria might appear to be—and might actually become—a form of anti-competitive collusion. Moreover, at the current stage of code development and public acceptance, an industry-wide approach is likely to be very disadvantageous to the companies that are seeking to develop creative, innovative responses to human and social concerns.

Independent Approach
I believe that for a company that is strongly committed to a substantive and effective code of conduct, a "go-it-alone" strategy is preferable at the present time. The direct economic benefits emanating from increased stakeholder trust, cooperation, and loyalty should provide ample incentive; and enhanced public reputation should translate into a more hospitable external socio-political environment over the long term. A go-it-alone company has the flexibility to fashion a code of conduct that takes advantage of its unique capabilities and to develop new systems and procedures of permanent value (and perhaps of market value to other firms as well). Successful individual firm experience may well permit the gradual development of multi-firm approaches.

Monitoring Council
Whatever the specific substantive content of a code of conduct, and whatever its level of sponsorship (division, corporate, or industry), its ultimate success depends upon the verification of its results by independent

S. Prakash Sethi

reviewers. I refer to these individuals as a "Monitoring Council." Such a Council should consist of three to five members with impeccable credentials for independence, knowledge, and, if possible, code formulation and implementation. The Council must have credibility with all constituent groups, including corporate directors and managers, governments, and other stakeholders. I do not believe that it is appropriate to include specific stakeholder representatives as Council members, since the Council's purpose is to determine the extent to which the company is meeting its public commitments, as expressed in its code. (Stakeholder representatives may well be included in consultations concerned with the drafting and revision of a code, which is a different matter.)

The principal task of a Monitoring Council should be oversight, with responsibility for verifying not only the results of field audits but, even more importantly, the company's responses to deficiencies when they are uncovered. Field monitoring of code compliance should be separated from verification and reporting, which should be the sole purview of the Council. The Council should develop a mechanism for receiving information and complaints about corporate performance from both within and outside the company. It should make regular public reports about the company's compliance with its code, and the content of these reports and the manner of their presentation should be the sole responsibility of the Council. The Council should, of course, make every effort to ensure that all facts in its reports are accurate, and that all conclusions are fully justified. Under the best of circumstances, the monitoring function should be viewed as a cooperative effort in which both the monitors and the corporation's field managers strive to ensure compliance. Under the worst of circumstances, where monitors and managers view each other as adversaries, the entire code implementation process will be a failure.

Mattel Experience

Mattel, the world's largest toy manufacturing company, announced the creation of its Global Manufacturing Principles (GMP) in November, 1997. The Code created a set of standards that would apply to all of the company-owned plants as well as those of its more than 300 primary contractor manufacturing facilities around the world. As part of its code formulation and implementation process, the company also committed itself to the establishment of an independent council to monitor its operations to ensure compliance with GMP. It is called the Mattel Independent Monitoring Council for Global Manufacturing Principles (MIMCO). To the best of my knowledge, it was the first time that a major multinational corporation voluntarily committed itself to independent monitoring by outside observers who had complete authority to make their findings available to the public.

In establishing the Council, Mattel was trying to identify itself as a socially responsible company and good corporate citizen. Mattel believed that it was important that its policies, operational procedures, and performance measures under the GMP should receive broad public recognition and acceptance. Mattel also considered it extremely important that the relevance and adequacy of the GMP, as applied to the company's overseas operations, particularly in developing countries, be recognized and accepted by its employees and managers worldwide.

The Council currently consists of three members: Dr. S. Prakash Sethi, Distinguished University Professor of Management, Zicklin School of Business, City University of New York; Dr. Murray Weidenbaum, Distinguished University Professor of Economics, Washington University in St. Louis, and a former chairman of the Council of Economic Advisors; and Dr. Paul McCleary, President and CEO of ForChildren, Inc., and former President and CEO of the Save the Children Foundation.

In accepting their assignment, Council members received a number of important assurances from the company's top management:

- Mattel will ensure that the code meets or exceeds all pertinent host country laws and best industry practices in the areas of its operations.
- The company is committed to the code and will devote the necessary resources to ensure compliance to it by field managers in the company's owned and controlled plants, and will cooperate and assist the company's major vendors to comply with the code.
- The company will create a highly objective, quantifiable, and outcome-oriented set of standards that will add substance and comprehensiveness to the code and ensure the code's implementation in a meaningful manner.
- The company will make every effort to work toward the enhancement of these standards in an evolutionary manner that will enhance the financial and social well-being of its workers, and also contribute to the economic growth of the countries involved.

During its first phase, MIMCO will focus its efforts on auditing those twenty or more plants that are owned or controlled by Mattel. These account for close to 70 percent of Mattel's world-wide production. A very large part of Mattel's production operations are based in the Asia-Pacific Region: Peoples' Republic of China, Indonesia, and Malaysia. This audit will therefore cover the topics that have been of major public concern in those areas: workers' health and safety, wages, and living conditions. We expect this phase of the audit process to be completed by April 1999, and our findings will be made public soon thereafter.

S. Prakash Sethi

An audit is only as good as the questions it asks and the activities and issues it covers. We have spent the last six months developing a highly objective, quantifiable, precise, and statistically rigorous set of instruments that will be used in conducting field audits. These will cover, among other things:

- Workers' environment, health and safety, and working conditions.
- Wages and working hours.
- Living conditions.
- Communications with the management concerning their living and working conditions, new employee orientation methods, and regular training programs.

Mattel has already completed extensive in-house audits to ensure that its own plants, and those of its major suppliers, are in compliance with GMP. Where necessary, it has also worked closely with the company's suppliers to help them improve their operations to meet Mattel's standards—frequently at Mattel's expense. And, in a number of cases, where suppliers have been unable or unwilling to make such an effort, Mattel has discontinued its business relationship with them. Mattel has established a single global task force with members located in its Asian Region headquarters in Hong Kong and in its corporate headquarters in El Segundo, California. This task force has been responsible for generating the necessary databases for Council use in creating audit protocols; these, in turn, will be used by the independent auditors appointed by, and reporting to, the Council.

Concluding Thoughts

The emerging global economic order of the 1990s has once again brought capitalism and its principal actor, the multinational corporation, to new levels of prominence and power. Unlike the 1960s, when multinational corporations were seen as a threat to national sovereignty and political freedom, the dominant contemporary view seems to be that the multinational corporation is—or certainly can be—an agent of positive change. However, beneath this veneer of hope and expectation, lies distrust in the unaccountability of the corporate behemoth and the fear of its potential for doing harm whether through misjudgment or abuse of power.

The contemporary tensions between business and society—which will certainly extend into the next millennium—do not arise from obvious conflicts between right and wrong, guilt or innocence. Their more subtle sources are, for example, alternative concepts and combinations of equity and inequity, the distribution of potential social and economic benefits, the virtue of frugality and the sin of undue accumulation, and the morality of principles versus the morality of situations. We realize that we live in an increasingly interdependent, global society where the welfare of the individual human being is deeply, and often unpredictably, embedded in the operation of the entire system. In this complex environment, we cannot pretend to separate moral principles from institutional practices, political power from economic influence, or human and environmental values from material wealth.

The large corporation must become an active agent for social change if it is to make the world safe for itself. Rules of law, democratic institutions, and the ethics of competition and the marketplace are requirements for the continued success of multinational corporations and, indeed, contemporary capitalism. The corporation can no longer pretend to be a reactive participant within the social system, responding (positively or negatively) to pressures and goals arising from other groups. As a dominant institution in society, it must accept responsibility for independent initiative, both with respect to its own goals and the formation of the public agenda. Effective participation requires that the corporation be able to articulate who and what it is from a social perspective, and what role its processes and products play in society. This articulation is, in fact, the ultimate purpose and result of a corporate code of conduct.

---

[1] The editorial work of Lee E. Preston on this paper is deeply appreciated.

S. Prakash Sethi

Corporate Responsibility: Comparative Analysis of Current Documents

Lee E. Preston and Danielle Mihalko, Robert H. Smith School of Business, University of Maryland

Introduction

This section summarizes a group of eleven documents, all originating or reissued during the 1990s, that express concern and offer guidance about corporate responsibility in the global economy. The documents analyzed vary greatly in character, but all of them are directed toward companies, and toward analysts and consultants who might seek to evaluate or improve the impact of business activity on humanity and society. An overwhelming majority of large corporations in North America, and many others elsewhere, have published "codes of conduct" of one kind or another, and many of the documents reviewed here refer to these codes for illustrative purposes. No company-level documents are, however, included in this survey. It is important to note that none of the documents reviewed here suggests that improved corporate social performance requires any expansion of regulation and control of corporations by units of government, although two of them—the International Labour Organisation (ILO) *Tripartite Declaration* (Document 1) and the North-South Institute study (Document 11)—emphasize the role of government in support of corporate activity.

The first eight documents, summarized in the Comparative Analysis Matrix, below, present or imply specific policies or codes of conduct that might be adopted and followed by individual companies. The remaining three documents included in the study do not fit this format. The report from the Prince of Wales Business Leaders Forum *(Business as Partners in Development;* Document 10) presents a broad perspective on corporate social performance and possibilities, with particular emphasis on operations in transitional societies. The North-South Institute study *(Canadian Corporations and Social Responsibility;* Document 11) is comparably broad, and stresses the importance of "projecting Canadian values," particularly in disparate cultural environments. The Motorola publication (*Uncompromising Integrity*; Document 9) emphasizes ethical dilemmas, with brief introductory chapters followed by case studies and commentaries. Review of these broad documents suggests that no matter how much attention firms and governments might give to developing and implementing performance guidelines, difficult problems will still arise from problematic cultural and environmental situations, as well as from human frailty.

Among the documents suitable for comparative analysis (and therefore included in the Matrix), the oldest is the ILO *Tripartite Declaration* (Document 1), first adopted in 1977, but periodically updated since that time and interlinked with many more recent ILO initiatives. Although this document originated during a period of international demand for greater government control over corporate activity, it is addressed as much to companies as to governments and recommends against many restrictive and protectionist government policies. Its primary emphasis is on employment and working conditions.

The employment relationship is also the principal focus of the *Guidance Document for Social Accountability 8000* (Document 2), recently developed by the staff of the Council on Economic Priorities (CEP). Devised as a tool for managers and analysts, the aim of this document is "to improve working conditions globally." Its detailed provisions give explicit substance to the broad guidelines presented in ILO and other more general publications.

The Caux Roundtable statement of 1994 (Document 3) recommends a transition in corporate thinking "beyond shareholders toward stakeholders," which is subsequently made more explicit in the Interfaith Center on Corporate Responsibility (ICCR) and Institute of Business Ethics (IBE) publications (Documents 4 and 5, respectively). The latter present extensive summaries and excerpts from other corporate and independent sources; the ICCR document takes the final step of combining ideas from various sources into a single set of guidelines.

The other three documents in the Matrix (Documents 7, 8, 9) arose from corporate sponsorships by Hitachi, Shell, and The Body Shop; they are not, however, conventional "company codes." Each of them displays a broad perspective and reviews a wide range of issues and implementation devices that might be relevant in many different corporate settings. Taken together, they suggest that some elements of the business community are more comfortable with a broad conception of satisfactory corporate performance than conventional corporate rhetoric and press coverage might indicate.

All of the documents under analysis express or imply the view that corporations should be managed in the interest of their "stakeholders."

Lee E. Preston and Danielle Mihalko

The ILO and SA 8000 statements (Documents 1 and 2, respectively) are limited to the concerns of employees; all of the others explicitly recognize multiple stakeholder groups. The Shell report (Document 8) recognizes five areas of stakeholder responsibility: shareholders, customers, employees, "those with whom we do business," and "society"; the Hitachi report (Document 7) devotes two chapters to "working with stakeholders worldwide," in addition to several chapters on "corporate citizenship." The North-South Institute study (Document 11) recommends "a systems-centered approach to stakeholder management" that includes "social systems and the natural environment" as well as conventional firm-centered stakeholder categories. Taken as a group, they offer both implicit and explicit support to the further development and implementation of "Principles of Stakeholder Management."

Comparative Analysis Matrix

Stakeholder Categories	Document 1 ILO	2 SA 8000	3 Caux	4 ICCR	5 IBE	6 Stakeholder Corporation	7 Hitachi	8 Shell
Employees								
Alcohol/Drug Abuse					x*		x	x
Child Labor		x		x				
Communication			x	x	x	x		x
Compensation	x	x	x	x	x	x		
Conflict of Interest				x	x*			x
Discipline	x	x				x		
Equal Opportunity/Discrimination	x	x	x	x	x*	x		x
Forced Labor		x		x				
Freedom of Association	x	x		x		x		
Health and Safety	x	x	x	x	x*	x	x	x
Human Rights	x	x	x	x	x	x		x
Insider Dealings					x*			
Integrity/Bribes/Gifts			x	x	x*			x
Management		x				x	x	
Political Choices/Contributions					x*	x		x
Sexual Harassment				x	x*	x		
Training and Education	x		x	x	x	x	x	x
Working Hours	x	x		x				
Competitors								
Free Competition			x	x	x*	x		x

*Report compares these areas over 10 identified companies

Lee E. Preston and Danielle Mihalko

Comparative Analysis Matrix (continued)

Stakeholder Categories	Document 1 ILO	2 SA 8000	3 Caux	4 ICCR	5 IBE	6 Stakeholder Corporation	7 Hitachi	8 Shell
Competitors, continued			x	x	x	x		x
Industrial Espionage					x			
Intellectual Property Rights			x		x			
Communities			x	x	x	x	x	x
Community Development			x	x	x	x	x	x
Donations			x	x		x	x	x
Government Authority			x		x	x	x	
Human Rights			x	x	x	x		x
Sustainable Development			x	x	x	x	x	x
Customers			x	x	x	x	x	x
Research Customer Needs						x		x
Health and Safety of Customers			x	x	x	x		x
Quality			x		x	x		
Truthful Advertising			x	x	x	x		
Environment			x	x	x*	x	x	x
Animal Welfare						x		
Climate Change				x				x
Consumption/Recycling				x	x	x	x	
Environmental Audit			x	x	x	x		x
Environmental Reporting			x	x		x		x

*Report compares these areas over 10 identified companies

Comparative Analysis Matrix (continued)

Stakeholder Categories	Document 1 ILO	2 SA 8000	3 Caux	4 ICCR	5 IBE	6 Stakeholder Corporation	7 Hitachi	8 Shell
Environment, continued			x	x	x*	x	x	x
Renewable Resources			x	x		x		x
Waste and Chemical Disposal				x	x	x		x
Stockholders/Investors			x	x	x	x		x
Apply Professional Management			x		x			
Communicate with Investors			x	x	x	x		
Investment Decisions			x			x	x	x
Transparent Finances			x	x	x*	x	x	
Wealth Maximization			x	x		x	x	
Suppliers			x		x	x	x	
Ethical Behavior by Suppliers			x	x	x	x	x	
Fairness/No Coercion			x		x	x		
Long-term Relationships			x		x	x	x	
Pay on Time			x		x	x		
Share Information			x		x	x		
Other			x		x	x		x
Globalization					x	x	x	x
Monitoring				x	x	x		x
Software Copying					x*			x
Transparency			x	x	x	x	x	x

*Report compares these areas over 10 identified companies

26   *Lee E. Preston and Danielle Mihalko*

Part 1:
Documents Described in the Matrix

Document 1: ILO

International Labour Office (ILO). 1991.

Tripartite Declaration of Principles Concerning Multinational Enterprises and Social Policy.

Geneva, Switzerland: ILO.

ISBN: 92-2-107100-6

Purpose and Focus

The *Tripartite Declaration of Principles Concerning Multinational Enterprises and Social Policy* was originally adopted by the Governing Body of the ILO in 1977 and reissued with updated information in 1991. The *Declaration* is a set of principles dealing with issues of employment, training, conditions of work and life, and industrial relations. It is directed toward governments, employer and worker organizations, and multinational corporations.

Surveys are conducted every three years to monitor to what extent governments, employer and worker organizations, and multinational enterprises are applying the declaration. A summary of the results of these surveys is submitted to the Governing Body.

This document is an original piece of work, as the contents of the declaration itself were researched by the ILO. The *Declaration* is a very formal document; no explanation of any section is offered, nor is background information provided. The document acknowledges that disagreement or misunderstanding may arise regarding its application. Fortunately, provisions have been made to handle such disputes, and a procedure was instituted in 1981, under which those in dispute may request the ILO to interpret the meaning of its provisions.

Summary

General Practices

- Governments, employer and worker organizations, and multinationals should respect:
  - the sovereign rights of States, obey national laws, consider local practices, and respect international standards.

- the Universal Declaration of Human Rights and the corresponding International Covenants adopted by the General Assembly of the United Nations.
  - the Constitution of the International Labour Organisation.
- Multinational enterprises should take into account established general policy objectives of the countries in which they operate.
- Governments should promote good social practice.

Employment
- Governments should pursue as a major goal an active policy to promote full, productive, and freely chosen employment. This is especially important in developing nations where unemployment rates are often very high.
- Multinationals should attempt to increase local employment opportunities and standards, taking into account local laws and practices.
- Multinationals should give employment priority to local workers rather than international workers.
- Multinationals should utilize, as often as appropriate, local contractors and suppliers.
- Governments should actively pursue policies that promote equal employment opportunity.
- Governments and multinationals should seriously consider the impacts that public policy and business decisions have on local employment. If decisions must be made that will negatively impact employees, reasonable notice should be provided to all workers.
- Multinationals should attempt to provide stable employment to local workers.
- Governments should provide income protection for workers whose employment has ended.

Training
- Governments should develop national policies for vocational training, closely linked with employment. Multinationals should fully support these programs, assisting when appropriate.
- Multinationals should ensure that relevant training is provided for all levels of employees.

Conditions of Work and Life
- Wages, benefits, and conditions of work offered by multinationals should be competitive with local standards.
- When an appropriate comparison does not exist, multinationals should provide the best wages, benefits, and working conditions within the framework of government policies.

Lee E. Preston and Danielle Mihalko

- Governments should adopt measures to ensure that lower income groups and less-developed areas benefit as much as possible from the activities of multinationals.

Safety and Health
- Governments should ensure that multinational and local enterprises provide adequate safety and health standards for their employees.
- Multinationals should maintain the highest standards of safety and health.
- Multinationals should cooperate with international organizations concerned with health and safety issues.

Industrial Relations
- Multinationals should maintain the level of industrial relations that local companies maintain.
- Workers should have the right to join organizations of their own choosing without prior approval.
- Organizations that represent workers should have adequate protection from interference.
- Where governments offer special incentives to attract multinationals, these incentives should not limit the workers' right to associate.
- Workers should have the right to representative organizations of their own choosing for collective bargaining purposes.
- All businesses should provide adequate facilities for representative organizations to assist in the development of collective bargaining agreements.
- Governments should provide representative organizations with relevant industry and country information to help lay out objective criteria in the collective bargaining process.
- Workers should have the right to submit grievances without suffering prejudice as a result. Workers should bear the right to have grievances examined utilizing appropriate procedures.

Obtaining the Document
International Labour Office
ILO Publications
CH-1211 Geneva 22, Switzerland
www.ilo.org

Document 2: SA 8000

Council on Economic Priorities Accreditation Agency. 1998.

Guidance Document for Social Accountability 8000.

New York: CEPAA.

Purpose and Focus

SA 8000 was developed by the Council on Economic Priorities Accreditation Agency and is modeled after the International Standards Organization (ISO) ISO 9000 and ISO 14000 standards for quality control and environmental management systems.

The purpose of SA 8000 is to improve working conditions globally. This document focuses on internal business practices. SA 8000 is an international standard with a strong international focus. Companies can be audited under SA 8000 guidelines allowing customers and the public to know if suppliers and subcontractors have received SA 8000 certification.

SA 8000 is focused exclusively on employment issues and the employee as a stakeholder. Although the issues focused on can apply to subcontractors and suppliers, SA 8000 does not attempt to deal with them as stakeholders. Instead, it includes them as one of the parties being audited. In short, stakeholders other than employees are not addressed. However, ISO 9000 does address quality issues which presumably would cover customers, suppliers, and investors. ISO 14000 focuses on the environment and may cover community issues as well. SA 8000 only covers community issues from the perspective that employees come from the community; it does not address the community itself as a stakeholder.

This is a unique piece of work in that it is a new audit standard. This document is very practical because it serves as a manual for companies that may wish to go through the audit to receive certification or for companies that simply want to see where they might stand.

Summary

This is not a report. It is a guide with specific examples and checklists that can be used as a manual for companies preparing for an SA 8000 audit.

The introduction explains the benefits and costs of an audit. The benefits include reputation improvement, enhanced product quality, and greater consumer and investor confidence. After an overview of the purpose of SA 8000 and definitions, the document addresses social accountability requirements. This part of the document is broken down into nine sections:

1. Child Labor
2. Forced Labor
3. Health and Safety
4. Freedom of Association
5. Discrimination

6. Disciplinary Practices
7. Working Hours
8. Compensation
9. Management

Each of these sections contain five to six parts:

1. SA 8000 requirements
2. Intent of SA 8000
3. Sample checklist
4. Objective evidence
5. Examples of corrective action requests
6. Background information (in some sections)

SA 8000 does a moderately good job of addressing the differences that arise among cultures. For instance, with the issue of working hours in the sample checklist, the first item is, "The work week does not exceed 48 hours or the country's legal maximum work week (whichever is less)."

After addressing each of the audit areas, the document focuses on specific guidelines for preparing for the audit, conducting the audit, post-audit activities, and the appeals and complaints process.

Preparing for SA 8000
There are requirements that a company must meet before it can be audited. Pre-assessment activities, such as explaining the nature of the audit to staff, defining the audit scope, complying with local laws, and consulting with interested parties such as trade unions, must be completed before the audit can take place. To be effective, the initiative must be company-wide, management-led, focused on prevention rather than detection, and centered on continuous improvement.

Post-Audit Activities
Once the audit has been completed, the company audited must establish, document, and maintain procedures to investigate the cause of non-compliant activities and determine corrective actions. Six months after the audit, the auditors will return for a surveillance visit to assess whether all minor non-compliance issues have been addressed. Training should be provided after the audit to all employees and managers to ensure that everyone understands the importance and purpose of the audit and the guidelines of SA 8000.

Obtaining the Document

Council on Economic Priorities Accreditation Agency
30 Irving Place
New York, NY , USA 10003
Tel: (212) 358-7697; Fax: (212) 358-7723
www.cepaa.org

Document 3: Caux

Caux Round Table. 1994.

Principles for Business.

Washington, DC: Caux Round Table Secretariat.

Purpose and Focus

The Caux Round Table is focused on corporate social responsibility, and its members believe that international business should play a central role in improving world economic and social conditions. The purpose of the *Principles for Business* is to set an international standard for measuring business behavior. The Round Table seeks to identify shared values, reconcile differing values, and develop a shared perspective on business behavior accepted and honored by all.

This is a small document, but even in its brevity it successfully covers many areas of corporate responsibility and stakeholder focus, which can be seen in the Matrix. However, each area is only touched upon quickly, and, although there is significant breadth to the document, depth is lacking.

Summary

Section 1: Preamble

- Business is becoming increasingly global.
- Laws are necessary, but insufficient, guides for conduct.
- Responsibility for policies and actions of business, and respect for stakeholders is fundamental.
- Shared values are as important for global communities as they are for local communities.

Section 2: General Principles

Principle 1: The Responsibilities of Businesses: Beyond Shareholders Toward Stakeholders

- Businesses have a role to play in improving the lives of their customers, employees, and shareholders by sharing the wealth they have created.
- Suppliers and competitors should expect businesses with which they work to be fair and honest.
- Businesses should play an active role in the future of the communities in which they operate.

Principle 2: The Economic and Social Impact of Business: Toward Innovation, Justice, and World Community

- Businesses in foreign countries should contribute to the social advancement of those countries by providing jobs and by raising the purchasing power of citizens.
- Businesses should contribute to human rights, education, welfare, and vitalization in countries where they operate.
- Businesses should contribute to the economic and social development of the world at large through efficient resource use, fair competition, and an emphasis on innovation.

Principle 3: Business Behavior: Beyond the Letter of Law Toward a Spirit of Trust

- Businesses should recognize that by being trustworthy, they not only increase their own credibility, but also add to the efficiency of business transactions on an international level.

Principle 4: Respect for Rules

- Businesses should respect international and domestic rules.
- Businesses should recognize that some behavior, although legal, may have adverse consequences.

Principle 5: Support for Multilateral Trade

- Businesses should support the General Agreement on Tariffs and Trade (GATT), World Trade Union, and other similar agreements.
- Businesses should cooperate to promote trade liberalization.

Principle 6: Respect for the Environment

- Businesses should protect and, when possible, improve the environment, promote sustainable development, and prevent the wasteful use of natural resources.

Principle 7: Avoidance of Illicit Operations

- Businesses should not participate in or condone bribery, money laundering, or other corrupt practices.
- Businesses should not trade in arms, drugs, or organized crime.

Section 3: Stakeholder Principles

Customers

- All customers should be treated with dignity.
- Customers should be provided with the highest quality of products and services.
- Customers should be treated fairly in all aspects of a transaction, including service and actions to rectify dissatisfaction.

- Businesses should ensure that the health and safety of customers will be sustained or improved through the use of a product or service.
- Businesses should respect human dignity and the culture of the customer in marketing and developing products.

Employees
Businesses should:
- Provide jobs that improve the living conditions of workers.
- Provide working conditions that respect the health and safety of workers.
- Be open and honest in communicating and sharing information with employees.
- Listen to and, when appropriate, act on employee suggestions.
- Engage in good faith negotiations when conflict arises.
- Avoid discriminatory practices.
- Promote internally the employment of people of differing abilities in the workplace.
- Protect employees from injury or illness in the workplace.
- Assist employees in developing transferable skills.
- Be sensitive to the unemployment problems faced as a result of business decisions.

Owners/Investors
Businesses should:
- Apply professional and diligent management to secure a competitive return on investment.
- Disclose relevant information.
- Conserve, protect, and increase investments.
- Respect investors' requests, suggestions, complaints, and formal resolutions.

Suppliers
Businesses should:
- Seek fairness and truthfulness in all activities including pricing, licensing, and the right to sell.
- Ensure that activities are free from coercion and unnecessary litigation.
- Foster long-term relationships with suppliers.
- Share information with suppliers and integrate them into planning processes.
- Pay suppliers on time and in accordance with agreed-upon terms.
- Utilize suppliers that respect human dignity.

Competitors

Business should:

- Foster open markets for trade.
- Promote competitive behavior that is socially responsible.
- Refrain from participating in questionable payments or favors.
- Respect intellectual property rights.
- Refuse to obtain information in a dishonest manner.

Communities

Business should:

- Respect human rights and dignity.
- Recognize the legitimate role of government and support public policies.
- Collaborate with local organizations working to improve the standard of living of the community.
- Promote sustainable development and conserve the environment.
- Support peace, security, diversity, and social integration.
- Respect the integrity of local cultures.
- Exemplify good corporate citizenship through charitable donations, educational and cultural contributions, and employee participation in community affairs.

Obtaining the Document

Caux Round Table Secretariat
1156, 15th Street, NW, Suite 910
Washington, DC, USA 20005
Tel: (202) 872-9077; Fax: (202) 872-9137
http://www.cauxroundtable.org/

Document 4:   ICCR

Interfaith Center on Corporate Responsibility. 1998.

Principles for Global Corporate Responsibility:
Bench Marks for Measuring Business Performance.

New York: ICCR.

Purpose and Focus

The purpose of the Principles for Global Corporate Responsibility is to promote positive corporate social responsibility consistent with sustaining the human community and all creation. This document is an accountability tool to evaluate companies, their codes of conduct, and code implementation.

In general, this is a useful document. It provides many examples of what various companies are doing and reproduces the guidelines for social responsibility of various organizations. The principles, criteria, and benchmarks are especially useful because they are specific, concrete, and easy to follow. However, the contents of this document are limited. A document with this format would be significantly larger if it incorporated all stakeholders and all issues that affect each group. There is little analysis in the report as it is mostly a reproduction of the Principles for Global Corporate Responsibility and other codes.

Summary

Part 1: Principles

The principles are broken down into sixteen sections:

1. Ecosystems
2. National Communities
3. Local Communities
4. Indigenous Communities
5. The Employed
6. Women in the Workforce
7. Minority Groups
8. Persons with Disabilities
9. Child Labor
10. Forced Labor
11. Suppliers
12. Financial Integrity
13. Ethical Integrity
14. Shareholders
15. Joint Ventures/Partnerships/Subsidiaries
16. Customers and Consumers

Each of the sixteen sections uses the same format, as follows:

1. Name of section (e.g., Ecosystems).
2. Principles: a set of general policy guidelines for each area.
3. Criteria: specific ideas for implementing the principles and achieving the overall section goal.
4. Benchmarks: concrete examples of actions that would contribute to the objectives.

Part 2: Glossary
A glossary of terms used in the document.

Part 3: Appendices
There are twenty-four appendices, including documents such as the Coalition for Environmentally Responsible Economies (CERES) Principles, Bellagio Principles, and the Amoco Canada Petroleum Company Ltd. Aboriginal Policy. These appendices are simply reproduced from the sources. They are not analyzed or discussed.

Obtaining the Document
The Interfaith Center on Corporate Responsibility
475 Riverside Drive, Room 550
New York, NY, USA 10115
Tel: (212) 870-2295; Fax: (212) 870-2023

Document 5: IBE

Webley, Simon. 1997.

Codes of Ethics and International Business.

London: Institute of Business Ethics.

ISBN: 0-9524020-5-X

Purpose and Focus

For ten years the IBE has advocated that every major company should have a detailed code of ethics. This report specifically focuses on the codes of ethics of multinational companies. The relationship between a company and its foreign subsidiaries, joint venture partners, and agents can often lead to considerable ethical dilemmas. According to IBE, following the laws of a foreign country is mandatory, but it is not enough, especially when dealing with issues that are cultural or religious in nature. This report specifically focuses on best practices in the area of ethics codes for companies doing business abroad.

This document is mostly a collection of information. There is little original thought. No conclusions are made, nor is it a scholarly work. However, it is practical in that it is easy to use and contains details on how various companies view and deal with ethical issues. It is a good guide.

Summary

It is important for every company engaged in international trade and investment to have a clear written policy on ethical standards to guide employees. There are three global forces that are increasing the need for such guidelines in international business:

1. Rapidly expanding world trade and investment (globalization).
2. The spread of global information and international accessibility of information as a result of the information technology revolution.
3. An increase in the awareness of moral issues as they relate to public life, including business behavior. The environment is a particular example.

Comparison of Codes of Ten Western Multinationals

The report lists thirteen issues. Under each issue, an excerpt from each company's code is given which shows how that company officially addresses the issue. This part of the report is simply a categorization of direct statements from each of the codes. It does not appear that an investigation inside any of the companies has been done or that any significant or new conclusions on how companies deal with stakeholders have been made. The value of this report is that the information has been collected and categorized.

The thirteen issues are:

1. Political activities
2. Health and safety
3. Gifts
4. Conflicts of interest
5. Insider dealing
6. Equal opportunity and discrimination
7. Alcohol and drug abuse
8. Sexual harassment
9. Disclosure of company information
10. Financial transactions
11. Fair competition
12. Environment
13. Software copying

In addition, the implementation of the codes in the corporation is addressed.

The ten companies are:

1. Shell
2. BP
3. Texaco
4. ICI
5. Caterpillar
6. Honeywell
7. Alcan
8. Standard Chartered Bank
9. British Airways
10. Northern Telecom

Three Codes of Principles

The report reproduces sections or the entirety of three codes of principles that have been developed by international business organizations. The codes often serve as a checklist of key issues and as a means of bringing uniformity of practice among multinationals. The three codes are:

1. International Chamber of Commerce Codes
2. Caux Roundtable: Principles for Business
3. Interfaith Declaration on International Business Ethics

Examples of How Three Multinational Corporations Approach Business Ethics

The three companies used as examples are:

1. ICI Polyurethanes
2. ESSO UK plc
3. Northern Telecom (Nortel)

Lee E. Preston and Danielle Mihalko

To show how ICI approaches business ethics, the report reproduces excerpts from the ICI code of practice. The code of practice consists of basic principles and business inducements. The business inducements section is further broken down into more specific sections, such as split commission and business with governments.

For ESSO, the summary of a speech delivered by the Chairman and CEO of ESSO UK is reproduced. The speech gives a few specific examples of how the company communicates with its stakeholders. For instance, he mentions a twenty-four hour hotline for employees who find it difficult to raise issues with their supervisors.

For Nortel, there is a two-page summary (apparently obtained from Nortel) that contains information on how the company began its business ethics program, who Nortel considers its stakeholders to be, and specific commitments to each of the stakeholders. The following is a summary of the Nortel information:

Customers
- Deliver high quality products and services now and in the future
- Treat fairly and honestly

Employees
- Treat with respect
- Provide fair and equitable employment
- Ensure workplace safety and health

Shareholders
- Provide long-term value
- Provide accurate and honest information

Suppliers
- Act fairly in choice
- Act honestly in transactions

Community/Society
- Contribute to the well-being of local communities
- Protect the environment
- Respect national and local laws

The Nortel section also addresses how the company measures performance. In addition to qualitative means, the company seeks quantitative means to measure performance, although it acknowledges that ethics cannot be reduced to numbers.

Obtaining the Document
The Institute of Business Ethics
12 Palace Street
London, United Kingdom SW1E 5JA
www.ibe.org.uk

Document 6: The Stakeholder Corporation

Wheeler, David and Sillanpaa, Maria. 1998.

The Stakeholder Corporation: The Body Shop Blueprint for Maximizing Shareholder Value.

London: Pitman Publishing.

ISBN: 0273-62661-2

Purpose and Focus

This book is an analysis of stakeholder management. The central theme is that the long-term value of a company depends on the knowledge, skills, and commitment of employees, and the company's relationship with customers, investors, and other stakeholders. The book presents best practices in stakeholder management from companies all over the world and argues that stakeholder inclusion leads to improved long-term business performance, including a better economic return for shareholders. This book does not take a moralistic approach or argue that stakeholder inclusion is right or wrong. It is written for those who are already convinced that a stakeholder focus is important. It lists specific reasons why inclusion of each of the stakeholders is necessary and then makes suggestions for how this can be done.

Summary

Parts One and Two of the book give an introduction to, and the history of, stakeholder management.

Part Three is a guide to stakeholder management. This section contains specific recommendations and suggestions on how to best include stakeholders in company activities. This section is broken down into many chapters, each with a specific focus. The first chapter focuses on the general approach to stakeholder inclusion. This chapter is then followed by the sections listed below. After each section, highlights from the chapter are listed.

Shareholders and Investors

- Structural and individual power should be balanced. In large companies the role of the chairman and the role of the CEO should be separate.
- Annual and other reports must be credible and meet the most rigorous standards of financial disclosure. They must provide enough commentary to allow readers to fully understand how the company is performing, financially and otherwise.

Employees and Managers
- A general human resources policy, a code of ethics, and an occupational safety and health policy are all essential for the stakeholder-inclusive company.
- With respect to remuneration, there must be transparency, fairness, and comparability.
- Companies can use the following quantitative measures of performance with respect to fair remuneration: ratio of top to lowest salary, ratio of top 10 percent of salaries to the lowest 10 percent, spread of eligibility for benefits.
- Companies must train their employees and communicate honestly with them. Employee morale is of the utmost importance to the company.
- Companies cannot discriminate in any way. To ensure a diverse workforce, a company must recruit from a diverse pool of applicants.

Occupational Safety and Health
- Companies must find out if safety legislation exists with which they must comply.
- Adequate emergency procedures must be in place, and employees must know that they exist and how they work.
- Safety policies must be properly documented and distributed.

Customers
- Information to customers must be truthful, clear, and relevant. Information given to customers should never be exaggerated, outdated, or misleading.
- Customers should be protected against all known and unknown risks of any product.
- Pricing should be clear. Companies that have gained a large share of the market should not use this to their advantage by raising prices and exploiting customers.

Quality
- Companies should be committed to quality improvement over the long term.
- Companies should give employees the proper training to improve quality consistently.

Suppliers and Business Partners
- Suppliers should ensure on-time and accurate delivery, price stability, after-sales service, and efficient paperwork.

The Local Community
- Straight financial donations should be separately administered, accounted, and reported as a percentage of pre-tax profits.
- If a company has a volunteering policy, it should be clearly and well communicated.
- Companies with expertise should share their knowledge and skills with local small businesses.
- Businesses should support schools by providing them with the materials and supplies that they need, not by donating product solely for marketing purposes.

Government and Civil Society
- Companies should conduct public policy initiatives in the open.
- Companies should not distort political party processes by making large donations.
- Companies should help government agencies that promote charitable, under-represented, or under-funded causes.

The Physical Environment and Non-Human Species
- Companies should be aware of, and comply with, relevant environmental legislation.
- Sustainable development policies should include minimizing consumption, ensuring social and economic fairness today and for the future, and practicing fair trade with developing countries.
- Companies should educate and communicate with employees and all stakeholders on why conservation of the environment is important.
- Animals should be used only when absolutely necessary. When they are used, they must be treated in a humane and ethical manner.

Transparency and Public Reporting
- Companies should be honest in their reporting.
- Companies should ask for feedback to understand whether or not they are meeting the needs of their stakeholders.

Obtaining the Document
Pitman Publishing
4720 Boston Way
Lanham, MD, USA 20706
Tel: (301) 731-9516

Document 7: Hitachi

Logan, David, Roy, Delwin, and Regelbrugge, Laurie. 1997.
Global Corporate Citizenship – Rationale and Strategies.
Washington, DC: The Hitachi Foundation.

Purpose and Focus

This document is a large study of the actions of multinational companies that are trying to define what global corporate citizenship means. No company is thoroughly analyzed. Instead, examples of specific actions are given where appropriate. Although the report is large and provides a wealth of information, the authors acknowledge that it does not cover everything. One of the goals of this report is to prompt further consideration, study, and thought on the subject. It asks, "What is corporate citizenship? Do I want to do this? How can I do this?"

This study argues that companies must be strategic in their philanthropic and charitable actions. It does not argue against the notion that "charity begins at home," but it does plainly state that "home" is now much more global and multicultural.

The term "corporate citizenship" in this report is intended to include other terms such as corporate responsibility, corporate community involvement, corporate community investment, and corporate community responsibility.

There are many reasons why companies strive to be good corporate citizens. These can include, among other reasons: maintaining or improving reputation, establishing contacts, finding marketing opportunities, or influencing the purchasing decisions of consumers. The motivation is unique for every company. The report states that all of these actions reinforce a company's commitment to corporate citizenship and should be encouraged, rather than looked at with suspicion.

Summary

Defining Global Corporate Citizenship

The report states that being a good corporate citizen implies that a corporation is "meeting, within reason, the expectations of all its societal stakeholders to maximize the company's positive impact and minimize the negative impact on its social and physical environment, while providing a competitive return to its financial stakeholders."

An interesting statement in this chapter explains why it is essential that multinational corporations be good global corporate citizens. "Capitalism depends on the presence of consumers, so capitalism's future depends solely on the system's ability, meaning companies' ability, to build the capacity of people to consume." The industrialized world has become saturated with producers. To maintain profitability and growth rates, companies must look to developing countries and must focus on increasing the consumption capacity in these areas.

Corporate Engagement Strategies
Strategic Business Interest
Based on corporate objectives, a company develops ideas internally, then works with a non-governmental organization (NGO) to implement actions.

Business/Community Partnerships
A company and community work with an NGO in a partnership to address specific critical issues.

Corporate Philanthropy and Corporate Giving
The decision-making process is largely within the corporation, or is handled by the corporation's foundation. Structures and finance schemes differ among companies and countries.

Several countries have tried to quantify corporate philanthropy and charitable giving, but have had little success in developing reliable estimates. Results of studies and the data available have not included marketing, advertising, service, equipment, employment, purchasing, and volunteer resources that benefit communities. If one utilizes the most accurate information, thus far, US corporate philanthropy is estimated at $7 billion per year. Internationally focused studies have shown that companies give most to education, and then to human and social services, arts and culture, the environment, and sponsorships.

Managing for Effective Corporate Citizenship
- Commitment by top-level executives is essential to the success of any corporate citizenship program.
- Corporate citizenship programs must be linked to business practices, and there must be clear management strategy to back up the commitment.
- Middle management must understand and be involved in corporate citizenship programs.
- To be effective, a corporate citizenship program must have the same status as other business programs such as market development or human resources development.
- The size of the company is not of high importance. Both large and small companies can develop good global citizenship programs.

The Global Competitive Framework: Differing National and Corporate Cultures, and Common Citizenship Needs

- The role of corporations in society is directly related to the role that governments play. In the US, taxes are lower and government is smaller than in western Europe or Japan. Because of its relatively small size, the US government has spent less money on social and economic development programs than other governments. This leaves more room for corporations to use profits for these types of programs.
- In Europe in recent years, corporations have been more involved in social programs than in the past. However, they have not given more money. Instead, they have mobilized non-cash resources. There is no one European tradition of corporate citizenship.
- Corporate citizenship programs must be adapted to the regulatory, cultural, and ideological structures of markets where multinationals intend to produce and/or market products.
- Although there is no one way, or most appropriate way, to be a good corporate citizen, all companies need to determine how they will interact with their stakeholders in each of the markets in which they operate.

Working with Stakeholders Worldwide

Employees and Shareholders

- Employees, not cash, are a company's largest and most valuable asset in the development of a corporate citizenship program.
- Not all shareholders are interested in the bottom line alone. Many recognize that there are economic consequences to irresponsible corporate actions.
- Partnering with a relevant association is one way to impact the training and recruitment of highly qualified employees. For example, Chevron wanted to employ more minority engineers. It therefore developed a long-term partnership with the African American Engineers Association. Chevron contributed cash as well as volunteers to serve as mentors. Over time, this encouraged African Americans to study engineering, and Chevron has been able to recruit employees from this pool of talent.
- Matched giving and volunteering programs enable employees to support local charities and community events.

Customers, Suppliers, and Communities

- Product price, service, and quality do not alone guarantee customer purchasing habits. Some consumers are also concerned with how the producer operates and how the product is made.

Lee E. Preston and Danielle Mihalko

- Corporate citizenship has been used as a marketing tool and should continue to be used as such. Customers often demand to know how a company operates, what it supports, and what customers will be supporting if they buy a product.
- Many customers are concerned with waste and the environment. Companies that are involved in environmental programs have marketed this to their advantage.
- Consumer education is a program that can benefit customers, communities, and companies in the long term.
- Choosing a supplier can often be a political decision. When a company makes a sourcing decision, it significantly impacts the job and economic prospects for the community that is chosen to supply.
- Communities look to businesses to provide jobs, taxes, and training, as well as to be good neighbors.

This report also contains a large chapter entitled, "Corporate Citizenship in Emerging Markets."

Obtaining the Document
The Hitachi Foundation
1509, 22nd Street, NW
Washington, DC, USA 20037
Tel: (202) 457 0588; Fax: (202) 296-1098

Document 8: Shell

Royal Dutch/Shell Group of Companies. 1998.

Profits and Principles – Does There Have to be a Choice?

London: Shell Group.

Purpose and Focus

This report is Shell's reaction to the growing public opinion that multinationals are responsible for their actions and impacts on society and the environment. Specifically, the public reactions to the executions of Ken Saro-Wiwa and eight Ogonis by Nigerian authorities in 1995, and Shell's plans to dispose of the Brent Spar offshore storage buoy in deep water in the Atlantic, caused the company to take a hard look at itself. Shell took an opinion poll and found that 50 percent of the people polled had a positive opinion of Shell, 40 percent had a neutral opinion, and 10 percent had a negative opinion. Shell thought that this 10 percent was a significant percentage, and decided that it must focus more on its care for the environment and human rights.

The tone of the report is one of atonement and honesty. The reader feels that Shell acknowledges that it lacks credibility with respect to its concern for stakeholders because of past actions but is trying very hard to gain this respect. Shell also acknowledges that this report is the first for the company, that it is incomplete and imperfect, but that it will improve in coming years. At the end of the report, the reader feels that Shell has indeed made significant internal changes toward a more stakeholder-focused way of doing business. Shell explains why it has made these changes (the public outcry mentioned above), and how it is making them. Shell also admits that wanting to do the right thing is not the same as actually doing it, and promises to act, not just talk. Shell states that company policies are only of value when there are rigorous procedures to make them work in practice.

Shell rarely uses the term "stakeholder" but its approach clearly is one that emphasizes the value and importance of taking into consideration the needs of stakeholder groups.

Summary

Social Responsibility Committee

The Social Responsibility Committee consists of six members of the boards of the parent companies of the Shell Group. The role of the committee is to review the policies and conduct of Shell companies with respect to Business Principles, Group Health, and Safety and Environment Policy and Commitment, as well as major issues of public concern.

Shell's Accomplishments in the Area of Stakeholder Management
1. Publishing of an introductory guide for managers on human rights.
2. Development of a guide on how to make oil and gas production more sustainable. Topics include:
   - Tools and techniques to contribute to sustainable development and their relationship to existing management systems.
   - Checklists for projects, health and social impact assessments, life cycle assessments, full-cost accounting.
   - Case studies on how to get started.
   - Policy making, target setting, consulting with stakeholders, minimizing impact on health, social structures and the environment, and building social capital.
3. Statement of General Business Principles Letter: Every year, all senior managers are required to sign letters covering performance in key areas of the Statement of General Business Principles, in particular, business integrity and health, safety, and environment (HSE). These letters are taken seriously, and each senior manager is personally held accountable for their content. In addition, many senior managers require their employees to sign similar letters on a "cascade" basis: a letter of representation, a letter of health, safety, and environment, and a letter of business principles.

List of Principles
In this section Shell addresses each of the following nine principles:

1. *Objectives:* Shell's objective is to engage efficiently, responsibly, and profitably in oil, gas, chemical, and other selected businesses and to participate in the search for and development of other sources of energy.
2. *Responsibilities:* Shell has responsibilities to shareholders (to provide good returns), customers (research to see what customers think of products), employees (equal opportunity, human rights, training), those with whom it does business (constructive long-term relationships), and society (taxes, employment, research and technical services, social investment and charitable giving, environmental laws).
3. *Economic Principles:* Although profitability is the key to economic success, investments must be made with an economic, social, and environmental concern.
4. *Business Integrity:* Shell must act with honesty, integrity, and fairness in all aspects of its business, and expects the same from those with whom it does business. Employees are assured that they will not be penalized if they lose business because they choose not to compromise Shell's principles.

5. *Political Activities:* Shell will not engage in payments to political parties, organizations, or their representatives, and will play no part in party politics. When dealing with governments and communities, Shell has an obligation to make its stand and opinion known on any matter that affects its stakeholders.
6. *Health, Safety, and the Environment:* Shell will utilize a systematic approach to health, safety, and environmental management. Shell sets targets for improvement, measurement, appraisals, and report performance.
7. *Community:* Shell will engage in societal matters that may not be directly related to the business. Involvement through community, educational, or donations programs will vary depending on the size of the company involved.
8. *Competition:* Shell companies support free enterprise. They seek to compete fairly and ethically and within the framework of applicable competition laws. Shell will not prevent others from competing freely with it.
9. *Communications:* Comprehensive corporate information programs provide full, relevant information about activities to legitimately interested parties, subject to the overriding considerations of business confidentiality and cost.

"Tell Shell"
There is a section in the report called "Tell Shell." Readers are encouraged to write their thoughts and ideas on the enclosed postcards and send them to Shell. Shell will publish the contents of the postcard on its website, if the writer consents.

Obtaining the Document
Shell International
Group External Affairs
Shell Centre
London, United Kingdom SE1 7NA
Tel: +44 (0) 171-934-5293; Fax: +44 (0) 171-934-5555
www.shell.com (Full report at: *http://download.shell.com/download/2872/*)

Part 2:
Documents Not Described in the Matrix

Document 9: Motorola

Moorthy, R.S., et al. 1998.

Uncompromising Integrity: Motorola's Global Challenge.

Schaumburg, IL: Motorola University Press.

ISBN: 1-56946-026-4

Purpose and Focus
This book focuses on the ethical issues that Motorola is, and will be, facing as its operations become increasingly global. Motorola believes that in order to be effective, its employees must be culturally sensitive and able to relate to people of diverse backgrounds. Motorola believes that this especially means that employees must deal with others in an ethical manner. Employees must understand not only the laws but the ethical values of the culture in which they are working.

One of the purposes of this book is to share the tacit knowledge that Motorola has acquired through the years regarding the reconciliation of the company's core ethical values with those of host cultures. The book attempts to address this question with a series of case studies that do not have correct answers, but instead encourage creative thinking about possible solutions and answers.

This book has been designed to be used by any individual interested in its contents, as well as an instructor or facilitator of a seminar on ethics.

Summary
The first three chapters of this book focus on the core ethical values of Motorola, approaches from anthropologists and other cultural scientists, and approaches from the field of ethics. The approaches are intended to provide Motorola employees with practical guidelines for dealing with ethical dilemmas.

The fourth chapter of this book is broken into twenty-four case studies. The cases are products of interviews with Motorola employees all over the world about situations that they or their colleagues in the company, or in a similar company, have encountered. The cases are therefore based on real situations, although the facts have been changed, and locations fictionalized, to ensure the anonymity of those interviewed. Each case is followed by a series of questions, as well as by commentary by two ethics experts. The following is a list of the case studies.

1. Uncompromising Integrity and Egregian Justice
2. The Phantom Air Ticket
3. "Nurturing" a Deal
4. Profits and People
5. Friendship or Mutual Bribery?
6. Constant Respect for—Human Rights?
7. When is Information "Proprietary"?
8. "Hardship" and the Eye of the Beholder
9. Personal Luxury or Family Loyalty?
10. Performance Bonuses: How to Allocate?
11. The Golf Clubs That Would Not Disappear
12. Are Training Budgets Geographically Equitable?
13. Rupert's "Royal" Gift
14. Facing Face
15. Just When is a "Tip" ONLY "To Ensure Promptness"?
16. Paying "Respect for People" in a Red Envelope
17. Is Motorola Its Agent's Ethical Keeper?
18. Operation Reap
19. The "Rights of the Monarch"
20. Gender Equity and the Eye of the Beholder
21. Purple Toenails
22. What Price Safety?
23. Phony Phones
24. A Tale of Two Cities

The book ends with a chapter on seven key conclusions to help the reader use and integrate the ideas of this book.

The book contains three appendices:

1. The Motorola Code of Conduct.
2. Excerpts from Motorola Japan's policy on giving and receiving gifts.
3. A guide to the twenty-four cases to help instructors determine which cases to assign for a class or learning group.

Obtaining the Document

Motorola University Press
1295 E. Algonquin Road
Schaumburg, IL, USA 60196
Tel: (847) 576-3142; Fax: (847) 576-7507
www.mot.com

Document 10: Business Leaders Forum

Nelson, Jane. 1996.

Business as Partners in Development.

London: The Prince of Wales Business Leaders Forum.

ISBN: 1-899159-94-0

Purpose and Focus
The Prince of Wales Business Leaders Forum is conducting a global learn-ing and networking initiative with the World Bank, the United Nations Development Programme (UNDP), and others, as part of the Partners in Development program. The program began in 1995 to identify, analyze, and promote good practices by businesses as partners in development. The goal is to encourage replication and wider implementation. The pro-gram looks at partnerships among businesses, government, and civil organizations. It focuses on the role that businesses can play in wealth creation, increasing economic opportunity, investing in human resources, and promoting environmental sustainability. The objective of this book is to present initial ideas and examples that will form the basis of this pro-gram.

Summary

The Case for Public-Private Partnership
Development Challenge
The development challenge of today is of great significance. There is a growing recognition that economic growth, human development, social cohesion, and environmental sustainability are all closely linked. There is also an awareness that these challenges cannot be met by governments alone and that business must be a part of the solution.

Corporate Challenge
Corporations are finding that globalization is increasing the competitive-ness of their markets. They must produce more efficiently and innovate better. At the same time, companies are finding that they are under more pressure than ever to be accountable to all of their stakeholders.

Benefits of Partnership
Multi-stakeholder partnerships give governments and businesses a tool to meet their mutual needs. "Successful partnerships can enhance and leverage corporate resources, reputation, relationships, and responsive-ness." They can also be catalysts for change and can bring about "effi-

cient, effective, and equitable solutions to the challenges of development."

The Contribution of the Business Sector
The business sector has the resources and capabilities to significantly contribute to development. Businesses can maximize the positive economic, social, and environmental spillover effects of their activities, and minimize the negative ones. Companies can become involved in public policy, make social investments, and engage in philanthropic activities.

Multi-Stakeholder Partnerships
Partnerships between International NGOs and Business
Some examples are:
- Conservation International and Intel
- CARE International and Starbucks Coffee

Partnerships between International Agencies and Business
Some examples are:
- The World Bank's Information for Development Program
- The UNDP's "Money Matters" Initiative

National Business Partnerships for Development
Some examples are:
- The National Business Initiative for Growth, Development, and Democracy in South Africa
- Philippine Business for Social Progress
- Business for Social Responsibility

Obtaining the Document
The Prince of Wales Business Leaders Forum
15-16 Cornwall Terrace, Regent's Park
London, United Kingdom NW1 4QP
Tel: +44 (0) 171-467-3600; Fax: +44 (0) 171-467-3610
www.oneworld.org/pwblf/

Document 11: North-South Institute

Hibler, Michelle, and Beamish, Rowena, eds. 1998.

Canadian Corporations and Social Responsibility: Canadian Development Report, 1998

Ottawa: North-South Institute.

ISBN: 1-896770-17-7; ISSN:1206-2308

Purpose and Focus

This is very much a macro-focused report. This document focuses on the policies of the Canadian government and how the government can better encourage and promote social and environmental responsibility. It has a strong international emphasis as well. The report is concerned with the responsibilities of Canadian firms operating in other countries. It is in other countries where firms must be more focused on social responsibility, since laws are often lenient or non-existent. In addition, the way Canadian firms behave overseas reflects significantly on the Canadian people as a whole.

This is not a manual or set of checklists, nor is it necessarily intended to be a resource for corporations to become more socially responsible. This report is intended to generate comments and interest in the subject of social responsibility in Canada. It is more academic than the other reports reviewed. It is also intended to inform. It is critical of the current policies of the Canadian government. This report is very thorough and in a macro sense covers all of the stakeholder areas. It clearly explains what a stakeholder is, why focusing on stakeholders is important, and how a focus on social responsibility can benefit corporations.

Summary

Why a Stakeholder Focus is Important

Self-interested behavior in the market system may not be in the best interest for society as a whole or for the natural environment. There are three reasons why corporations should move past a focus on the bottom line only:

1. The business world is embedded with social and natural systems. Corporate activity affects much more than just the bottom line. Business affects and shapes society in positive and negative ways.
2. The marketplace by itself cannot resolve environmental and social issues. Corporate actors engaged in trade and commerce are often unwilling or unable to influence social and environmental concerns in foreign countries.

3. It pays to be responsible. Corporate image is linked to profits. There is an important link between ethics and the perceived value of the firm. Studies show that unethical corporate behavior affects stock performance negatively.

How Can Companies Incorporate Social Responsibility Into Daily Operations and International Management Practices?
1. By integrating ethics into business practices.
2. By adopting a stakeholder approach. The firm's long-term interests must take into account the welfare of all its stakeholders.
3. By adopting an international code of conduct that addresses social and environmental inequities.
4. By broadening accountability for actions and unintended consequences.

Canadian firms doing business abroad are ambassadors for Canadian values whether or not they want to be. How they deal with their stakeholders, including the host government, and how they demonstrate their respect for the natural environment, sends a message to the host country about what Canadians think is important.

This report looks at the practices of the following five industries, and what each of them can do to be more socially responsible:

1. Financial services
2. Manufacturing
3. Mining, exploration, development, and production
4. Infrastructure and engineering
5. Management consulting

Canadian Operations Overseas

The Canadian Government Can Contribute to the Success of Canadian Corporations Overseas
The promotion of Canadian prosperity is the principal objective of most Canadian policies and programs. In foreign policy, trade missions have been at the top of the government agenda. During the past five years the government has taken a number of steps to foster Canadian business success abroad. However, trade with the fastest growing markets has been declining, and dependence on the US is increasing.

Ethical Behavior
Encouraging corporations to engage in ethical behavior is not only an issue for the private sector: it requires the active participation of both governments and individuals.

Lee E. Preston and Danielle Mihalko

The International Code of Ethics for Canadian Businesses
"Canadian business has a global presence that is recognized by all stakeholders as economically rewarding to all parties, acknowledged as being
ethically, socially, and environmentally responsible, welcomed by the
communities in which we operate, and that facilitates economic, human
resource, and community development within a stable operating environment."

The Growing Role of Private Foreign Investment in Development
The increase in private investment flows to developing countries from
Canada has been dramatic. Corporations have actively entered new and
expanding markets. At the same time, government funding for developing countries has declined. Private foreign investment will not be a per-
fect substitute for foreign aid, but will, instead, complement public funding.

Long-Term Wealth
Socially responsible firms can enhance long-term wealth by increasing
employee commitment, building customer loyalty, generating cooperation among suppliers and subcontractors, differentiating themselves
from the competition, and by lowering recruitment and labor costs.

**Commonalties Among Firms Consistently Demonstrating Social
Responsibility**
- Strong, progressive senior management.
- Responsible corporate practices, leading to competitive advantage
  in the marketplace.
- Act as catalysts for social change by filling unmet social needs.

Obtaining the Document
Renouf Publishing Co. Ltd.
5369 Canotek Road
Ottawa, ON, Canada K1J 9J3
Tel: (613) 745-2665; Fax: (613) 745-7660
www.renoufbooks.com